ONE INCREDIBLE DOG!

Lady

Written by Chris Williams
Illustrated by Judith Friedman

Published by Moo Press, Inc.
Warwick, New York

The text of this book is set in 16 point Adobe Bookman, with drop caps in Brush Script MT. Cover and book design by Judith Friedman. The illustrations are done in graphite with watercolor accents.

BVG 10 9 8 7 6 5 4 3 2

Library of Congress

Cataloging-in-Publication Data

Williams, Chris.

One Incredible Dog! Lady/Chris Williams; illustrated by Judith Friedman.

p. ; cm.

Summary: Readers join nurse Kathy and therapy dog Lady to learn about the good things therapy dogs do for people every day.

ISBN 0-9724853-3-3

[1. Dogs—Therapeutic use—Juvenile literature.

2. Working Dogs—Juvenile literature.

3. Dogs—Training—Juvenile literature.]

I. Friedman, Judith. II. Title.

RM931.D63 W55 2004   2003111728

636.7/088—dc22   0405

For information on permissions to reproduce, or about this and other Moo Press titles, please email info@MooPress.com or write to Moo Press, Inc. PO Box 54 Warwick, NY 10990. To order copies of this book, please visit our website at www.MooPress.com or your local bookstore. For more information on therapy dogs, contact either Therapy Dogs International at www.TDI-DOG.org or Delta Society at www.DeltaSociety.org.

Manufactured in the United States of America.

Published by Moo Press, Inc. Warwick, New York.

Dedicated to the memory of Grandma Teague, my best friend, and an above average bowler.

— C.W.

With all my heart,
to all those remarkable,
devoted animals!

— J. F.

"C'mon Lady! Time to go to work!" says Kathy.

Wagging her tail, Lady runs into the kitchen.

Kathy is a nurse.

Kathy and Lady work at hospitals and nursing homes.

Today they are going to work at a hospital.

Kathy puts colored neckerchiefs on Lady to help make people smile. After tying a bright red one on Lady, they are ready to go to work.

Lady is a special kind of a dog.

She is a certified "therapy dog."

Therapy dogs help sick and hurt people feel better.

How? Mostly by being a friend to them.

Not all dogs can be therapy dogs.

Therapy dogs must be very, very, VERY gentle.

They need to enjoy being around all kinds of people:

> young folks,

> old folks,

> and not-so-old but not-so-young folks.

A dog that tends to growl, even a little bit, wouldn't make a good therapy dog. Therapy dogs can't be "biters" either.

Therapy dogs are trained to obey their handlers at all times.

A naughty dog might upset or hurt a sick person.

When Kathy and Lady arrive at the hospital, several patients are in the halls outside their rooms.

Some stand with the help of walkers.

A few sit in wheelchairs.

One little girl gets around using crutches.

"Lady's here!" a patient announces excitedly.

Soon Kathy and Lady are surrounded by patients.

Everyone wants to pet Lady.

She doesn't mind being touched by so many people.

"Please have her do a trick," the little girl on crutches says.

"OK," Kathy replies.

Kathy snaps her fingers to get Lady's attention. Lady perks her ears to listen.

"Roll over," Kathy says. Lady obeys at once.

"Good girl," Kathy says and pats Lady's head.

Lady wags her tail.

The patients clap their hands and smile.

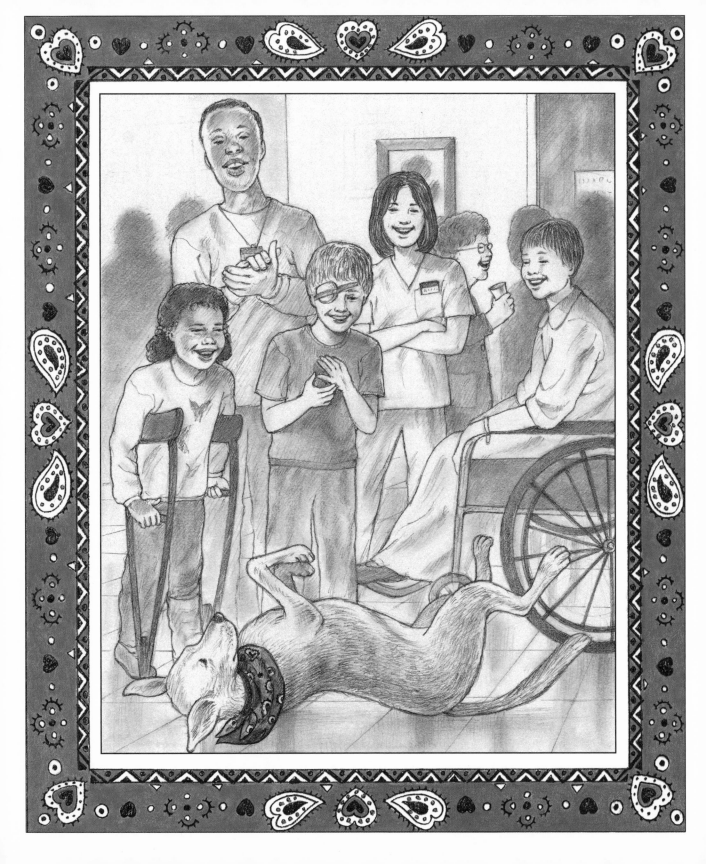

Lady knows many more tricks. Kathy has been teaching her tricks and how to obey since Lady was a puppy.

When Lady was six months old, Kathy would take her to the park and work on her obedience skills.

Kathy would say sit, and Lady would sit.
Kathy would say stay, and Lady would sit still, waiting for Kathy's next command.

Lady's favorite game was "fetch." Kathy would say sit, stay. Then, she would walk a few feet away and throw the ball.

Lady's tail would wag in excitement, but she knew that part of the game was to wait until Kathy said fetch.

"Fetch!" Kathy would command, and off Lady would run to retrieve the ball.

Today, there is lots of work to do!

Kathy needs to help many patients throughout the day.

Most people like dogs.

Some don't.

Lady only visits the patients she knows she's allowed to visit.

Lady is going to visit someone now. On the way, they pass by Doctor Wilson.

"Hi Kathy. Looks like Lady has her basket of balls and is ready to go to work." says Doctor Wilson.

"Yes," Kathy responds, "she has a ball at work every day."

The next stop is Mrs. Snow. Mrs. Snow holds out a rubber ball. "Fetch," she says, and rolls the ball on the floor. Lady runs after the ball, picks it up, and brings it back to Mrs. Snow. "Good girl!" says Mrs. Snow.

Again Mrs. Snow says, "Fetch," and rolls the ball across the floor. Lady brings it back to Mrs. Snow. Together, they play this game until Mrs. Snow's arm is tired. But she doesn't mind. Playing ball with Lady is fun, and it helps strengthen her arm.

When Kathy gets to room 127, the door is open a little bit.
Kathy peeks in and sees a new patient.

Kathy sees on the door that his name is Charlie.
He fell off his skateboard and broke his leg.
Kathy has heard from the other nurses that he doesn't like being in the hospital.

Kathy softly taps on the door.

    Knock-knock.

Charlie doesn't answer, so she knocks a little harder.

    Knock-knock.

"Who is it?" Charlie asks gloomily.

"Hi, I'm your nurse, Kathy." she replies.
"Is there anything I can do for you?"

"I just want to go home," Charlie says.
But when he sees Lady, his eyes get really big.
"A dog? In here? Cool!" he exclaims.
A smile crosses his face.

"Yes. Her name is Lady," Kathy replies.

"Come here, girl!" Charlie calls out.
Lady walks over to the side of the bed.
Charlie pats her head, and his smile gets bigger.

"Does she know any tricks?" Charlie asks.

"Yes," Kathy answers and snaps her fingers.
 "Lady, pray for Charlie," she commands.

Immediately, Lady puts her front paws together on the bed and bows her head.

"Wow! That's one incredible dog!" Charlie exclaims.
"That's for sure," Kathy replies.

After Kathy pours Charlie a cup of ice water and fluffs up his pillow, she and Lady go to visit other patients.

Kathy's next stop is to see Mr. Evans. He had a hip replacement and needs to walk a little bit more every day.

"Time to take a stroll," Kathy says.

"Is Lady going with us?" Mr. Evans asks.

"Of course!" Kathy answers.

"Great!" says Mr. Evans.

Kathy carefully helps him out of bed.

Together, they walk down the hall and back again.

Mr. Evans talks to Lady as he walks. She makes exercising fun.

When they return to his room, Kathy helps Mr. Evans back into his bed.

"See you tomorrow!" Mr. Evans says as Kathy and Lady move on to visit other patients.

Later in the day, Lady visits with little Rosie for awhile.

Rosie is very weak and sick from chemotherapy.
She doesn't feel much like getting out of bed.

All Lady does is keep her company.
But that's enough.

Soon, the work day comes to an end.
Kathy says softly, "C'mon, Lady. Time to go home."
Lady carefully crawls out of Rosie's bed. Quietly, she and Kathy leave the room.

As they head for the door, Kathy hears a voice call out,
 "Lady! Wait!"

Kathy turns and sees Emily hobbling towards them.
Emily had been in a car accident.

"I'm going home today!" she announces.
"Great!" Kathy responds.

"Would it be OK if I give Lady a special thank you?" Emily asks.
"She kept me company while I learned how to walk again."

"Sure," Kathy replies.

Emily sits down on a nearby chair and calls Lady over.

"I love you," Emily says as she leans over and hugs Lady.

And as if to say "I love you too," Lady wags her tail and snuggles close to Emily.

For Kathy and Lady, this is the best kind of thank you!

Hospitals aren't the only places you can find therapy dogs like Lady. These loving animals are also helping people in places like nursing homes, schools, and special homes for children. Therapy dogs also helped many people in New York and Washington, D.C. after the attacks of 9-11-01.

If you'd like to learn more about therapy dogs, here are two nonprofit organizations that can provide you with more information:

Therapy Dogs International
88 Bartley Road
Flanders, NJ 07836
www.TDI-DOG.org

Delta Society
580 Naches Avenue, SW Suite 101
Renton, WA 98055-2297
www.DeltaSociety.org